Usborne
Sticker Dolly Dressing
Rainbow Unicorns

Illustrated by Antonia Miller
and Johanna Fürst

Written by Fiona Watt

Contents

Unicorn forest

As the sun shines brightly and raindrops fall gently, a brilliant rainbow appears in the sky. Far below, unicorns emerge from the shelter of the trees to meet the fairies, Kai, Ariella and Sweetpea.

Kai

Ariella

Sweetpea

Juniper

Racing in the wind

Willow and Elvina love riding their unicorns as they gallop across the sky. The fairies hold tightly as the wind streams though the unicorns' manes and tails. Soon, more unicorns appear to join in the fun.

Willow

Sunbeam

Elvina

Larkspur

Woodland clearing

It's early on a misty morning. Selena, Posy and Faye have tiptoed into a secluded clearing, to watch a mother unicorn and her young foal sip refreshing water from a still, clear pool.

Selena

Dewdrop

Isy

Faye

Milkweed

Sunny meadow

As the sun rises in the sky, Aria and Hester decorate Skylark and Cowslip with fresh flowers that they have gathered from the meadow. They've made garlands for their hair and added flowers to their own clothes.

Aria

Skylark

Hester

Cowslip

Fairy wishes

Every evening, as the sun is setting, Princess Zarina, a woodland fairy, greets the Rainbow unicorns who come to ask for her help. She sprinkles them with fairy dust as she whispers magic wishes.

Harmony

Princess
Zarina

Castle in the clouds

The air is filled with shimmering wings as fairies flutter and twirl among the clouds. Unicorns, with bright flowing manes, emerge from the castle stables to leap and prance around the fairies.

Dewberry

Pippin

Aviva

13

Crystal cave

As Cosmo and Alora tiptoe quietly into an underground cave, crystals glisten and twinkle all around them. They are surprised to discover a family of unicorns that are resting in the cool air.

Moonstone

Cosmo

Alora

Secret orchard

Hidden away in the garden of a fairy palace, there's a magical orchard. Birds swoop among the branches of the trees, which are laden with delicious, sweet-smelling fruit.

Sorrel

Dillan

Marigold

Rosina

Elida

Moonlit lake

Stars twinkle in the night sky as Melody sings sweetly,
Nova plays a wooden flute and Celeste strums her fairy mandolin.
Unicorns gradually appear, entranced by the soothing sounds.

Melody

Starlight

Celeste

Nova

Northern lights

Snowflakes tumble through the cold, clear air,
as Astra, Lucio and Ilona, and their unicorn
Moonflower, gaze in wonder at the spectacular
lights dancing across the starry sky.

Moonflower

Astra

Lucio

Ilona

Feeding time

A group of unicorns stamp their hooves impatiently, as they stand in the early morning sunlight. They are waiting for the fairies to bring baskets of tasty things to eat and buckets of refreshing water.

Ambrosia

Lark

Gala

Briar

Sweet dreams

As night falls, Shadow, the unicorn,
has settled down in a quiet woodland to rest.
Snuggling into his soft, warm body, Alina has
drifted off to sleep, dreaming sweet fairy dreams.

Shadow

Alina

First published in 2023 by Usborne Publishing Limited, 83-85 Saffron Hill, London EC1N 8RT, United Kingdom. usborne.com
Copyright © 2023 Usborne Publishing Limited. The name Usborne and the Balloon logo are registered trade marks of Usborne Publishing Limited.
All rights reserved. No part of this publication may be reproduced, stored in a retrieval system or transmitted in any form or by any means
without prior permission of the publisher. First published in America 2023. UE.

Unicorns hiding in the forest

Ariella's headdress

Flowers for Juniper's mane

Garland for Juniper's back

Kai's outfit

Put Ariella's skirt on before her top.

A garland for his neck

Kai's boots

Sweetpea's headdress

Ariella's boots

Put Sweetpea's skirt on before her top.

Sweetpea's shoes

Willow's
blue top

Willow's
headdress

Willow's skirt

A garland for
Sunbeam's head

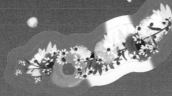

A garland for
Larkspur's head

Elvina's
headdress, top
and skirt

Clouds to decorate
the sky

Woodland clearing

Flowers for
Selena's hair

Selena's top
and skirt

Posy's
headdress

Posy's
outfit

Faye's
headdress
and dress

Dewdrop's
saddle cloth

A garland for
Dewdrop's
head

A garland for
Milkweed's
back

Flowers for Skylark's head and body

Aria's headdress

Hester's outfit

Cowslip's headdress

Aria's skirt and top

Hester's boots

Aria's boots

Flowers for Cowslip's neck and back

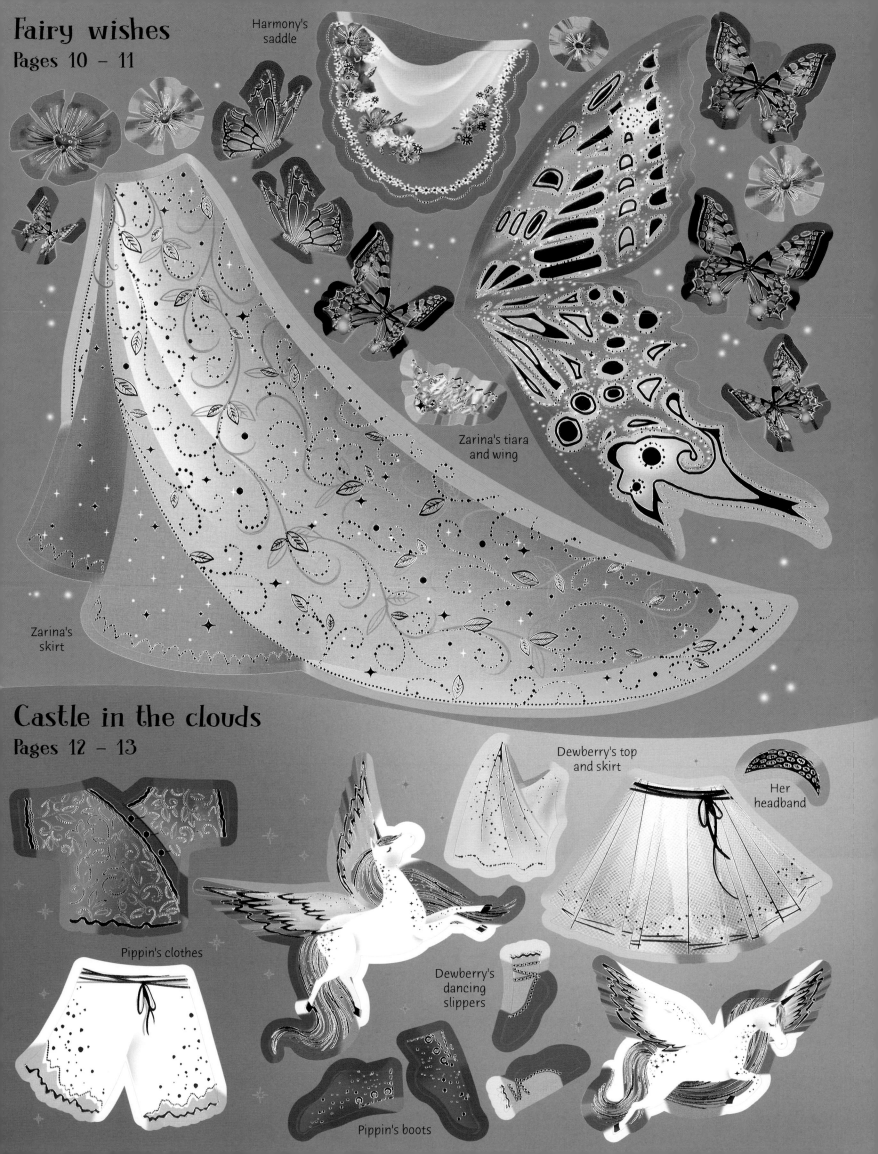

Fairy wishes
Pages 10 – 11

Harmony's saddle

Zarina's tiara and wing

Zarina's skirt

Castle in the clouds
Pages 12 – 13

Dewberry's top and skirt

Her headband

Pippin's clothes

Dewberry's dancing slippers

Pippin's boots

More stickers for
Castle in the clouds
Pages 12 - 13

Aviva's dress and tiara

Aviva's boots

Crystal cave
Pages 14 - 15

A garland for Moonstone's back

Bats hang from the roof of the cave.

Alora's outfit

Put Cosmo's bottoms on first.

Opal and Amber are Moonstone's foals.

Secret orchard

Garlands for Sorrel's head and neck

Marigold's outfit

Put Dillan's bottoms on before his top.

Rosina's headdress

Elida's headdress

A basket for Elida to hold

Dillan's boots

Rosina's clothes and shoes

Elida's skirt and fairy shoes

Moonlit lake

Flowers for Melody's hair

Melody's top

A garland for Starlight's neck

Put Melody's skirt on first.

Moon

Celeste's headdress

Nova's headdress, slippers and skirt

Celeste's mandolin

Celeste's skirt and slippers

Astra's headdress

Astra's outfit

Moonflower's blanket

Lucio's glove

Ilona's headdress

Ilona's top and skirt

Put Lucio's bottoms on before his top.

Lucio's boots

Ilona's snowboots

Feeding time
Pages 22 – 23

Flowers for
Ambrosia's
head

Ambrosia's
saddle cloth

Lark's top
and bottoms

Lark's
boots

Gala's and Briar's
headdresses

Gala's skirt
and boots

Sweet dreams
Page 24

A garland
for Shadow's
head

Alina's
skirt